DOOR & WINDOW
ESSENTIALS

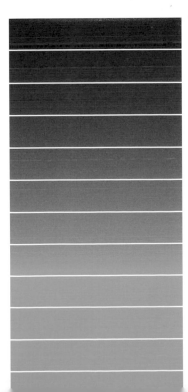

COWLES
Creative Publishing

A Division of Cowles Enthusiast Media, Inc.

Credits

Copyright © 1997
Cowles Creative Publishing, Inc.
Formerly Cy DeCosse Incorporated
5900 Green Oak Drive
Minnetonka, Minnesota 55343
1-800-328-3895
All rights reserved
Printed in U.S.A.

COWLES
Creative Publishing
A Division of Cowles Enthusiast Media, Inc.

President/COO: Nino Tarantino
Executive V.P./Editor-in-Chief: William B. Jones

Created by: The Editors of Cowles Creative Publishing, Inc.,
in cooperation with Black & Decker. **BLACK&DECKER** is
a trademark of the Black & Decker Corporation and is
used under license.

Printed on American paper by:
Quebecor Printing
99 98 97 96 / 5 4 3 2 1

COWLES
Enthusiast Media

President/COO: Philip L. Penny

Books available in this series:

Wiring Essentials
Plumbing Essentials
Carpentry Essentials
Painting Essentials
Flooring Essentials
Landscape Essentials
Masonry Essentials
Door & Window Essentials
Roof & Siding Essentials
Deck Essentials
Porch & Patio Essentials
Built-In Essentials

Contents

Most windows and doors are prehung units designed for easy installation. They are available in a vast range of styles and finishes. The units are preassembled, and trim moldings are either preattached or packed with the unit. Metal hardware is included with all window units, and with some doors. Top-quality windows and doors usually must be special ordered, and require two to four weeks for delivery.

Doors and windows link your home to the outside world and are the most important design elements in any remodeling project. Adding new windows makes your home brighter and makes living spaces feel larger. Replacing a shabby entry door can make your home more inviting to guests and more secure against intruders.

When planning your remodeling project, remember that the choice and placement of doors and windows will affect your life-style. For example, installing a large patio door is a good way to join indoor and outdoor living areas, but it also changes the traffic patterns through your house and affects your personal privacy.

In addition to style, consider the size and placement of windows and doors as you plan the project. Most homeowners install new windows to provide a better view, but remember that a well-positioned window also can reduce heating and cooling bills by serving as a passive solar collector in the cooler months and by improving ventilation in the summer.

Choose new doors and windows that match the style and shape of your home. For traditional home styles, strive for balance when planning windows and doors. In the colonial-style home shown on the left, carefully chosen window units match the scale and proportions of the structure, creating a pleasing symmetry. In the home on the right, mismatched windows conflict with the traditional look of the home.

Tips for Planning Door & Window Installations

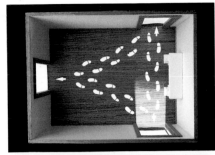

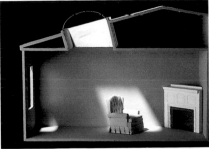
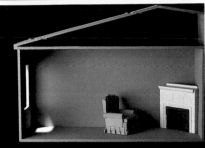

Traffic patterns through the home are determined by the placement of doors. Rooms with many doors seem smaller because traffic patterns consume much of the available space (top). When planning room layout, reserve plenty of space for doors to swing freely.

Divided window panes in windows and patio doors lend a traditional appearance to a home, and help create interesting lighting patterns in a room. Snap-in grills (shown), available for most windows and doors, are an inexpensive way to achieve this effect.

Consider the effect of sunlight when planning window positions. For example, when installing a skylight, choose a location and build a shaft to direct sunlight where you want it.

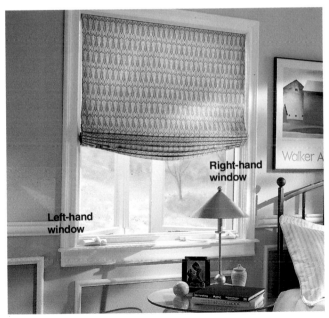

Left-hand window

Right-hand window

Right-hand vs. left-hand: Doors and casement windows are available in both right-hand or left-hand models, and this swing direction must be specified when ordering the units. When opened away from the operator, right-hand units swing to the right, left-hand units to the left. Double window units often have one right-hand and one left-hand unit. If you are installing a single window, choose a model that will catch prevailing breezes when it is opened.

Window combinations can be custom-ordered from the manufacturer. Unusual shapes, like the casement window with attached round top shown here, work well in contemporary-style homes, and also can help create a visual accent in a traditional-style home.

Door Styles

Interior panel doors have an elegant, traditional look. They are very durable and provide good soundproofing.

Interior hollow-core prehung doors have a contemporary look, and are available in many stock sizes. Hollow-core doors are lightweight and inexpensive.

Decorative storm doors can improve the security, energy efficiency, and appearance of your entry. A storm door prolongs the life of an expensive entry door by protecting it from the elements.

Entry doors with sidelights brighten a dark entry hall, and give an inviting look to your home. In better models, sidelights contain tempered, double-pane glass for better security and energy efficiency.

Sliding patio doors offer good visibility and lighting. Because they slide on tracks and require no floor space for operation, sliding doors are a good choice for cramped spaces where swinging doors do not fit.

French patio doors have an elegant appearance. Weathertight models are used to join indoor and outdoor living areas, while indoor models are used to link two rooms. Because they open on hinges, your room design must allow space for the doors to swing.

Window Styles

Casement windows pivot on hinges mounted on the side. They are available in many sizes, and in multi-window units that combine as many as five separate windows. Casement windows have a contemporary look, and offer an unobstructed view and good ventilation. They work well as egress windows.

Double-hung windows slide up and down, and have a traditional appearance. New double-hung windows have a spring-mounted operating mechanism, instead of the troublesome sash weights found on older windows.

Awning windows pivot on hinges mounted at the top. Awning windows work well in combination with other windows, and because they provide ventilation without letting moisture in, they are a good choice in damp climates.

Sliding windows are inexpensive and require little maintenance, but do not provide as much open ventilation as casement windows, since only half of the window can be open at one time.

Skylights introduce extra light into rooms that have limited wall space. Skylights serve as solar collectors on sunny days, and those that also can be opened improve ventilation in the home.

Bay windows make a house feel larger without expensive structural changes. They are available in dozens of sizes and styles.

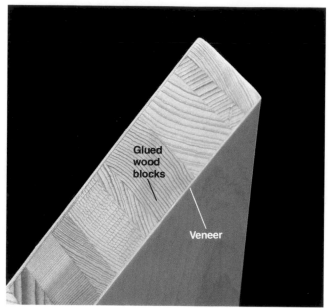

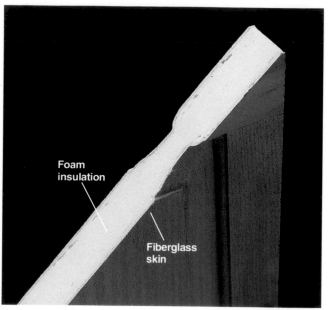

Look for "core-block" construction when choosing exterior wooden doors. Core-block doors are made from layers of glued or laminated wood blocks covered with a veneer. Because the direction of the wood grain alternates, core-block doors are less likely to warp than solid-core doors.

Fiberglass doors are expensive, but they are sturdy, have excellent insulating values, and require little maintenance. The fiberglass surface is designed to have the texture of wood and can be stained or painted different colors.

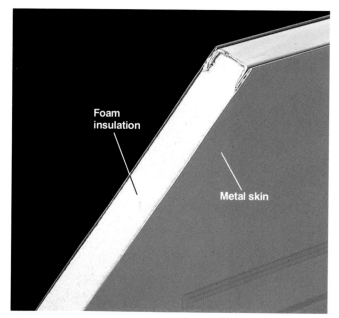

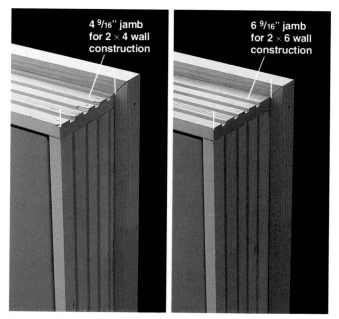

Steel entry doors are well insulated and have tight-fitting magnetic weather seals. Steel doors are less expensive than wooden doors and require little maintenance.

Check wall thickness before ordering doors and windows. Manufacturers will customize the frame jambs to match whatever wall construction you have. Find your wall thickness by measuring the jamb width on an existing door or window.

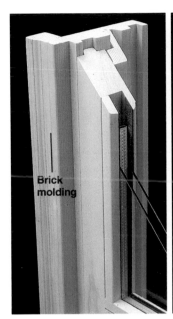  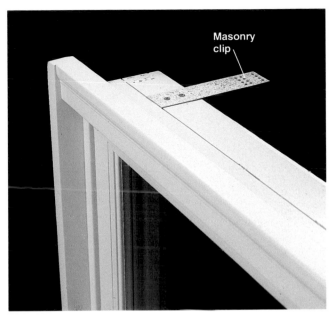

Wood-frames (left) are a good choice for windows and patio doors used in remodeling projects. Their preattached exterior brick moldings blend well with the look of existing windows. **Clad-frame** windows and doors (right) feature an aluminum or vinyl shell. They are used most frequently in new construction, and are attached with nailing flanges (page 77) that fit underneath the siding material.

Polymer coatings are optional on some wood-frame windows and doors. Polymer-coated windows and doors are available in a variety of colors, and do not need painting. To avoid using casing nails, which would pierce the weatherproof coating, you can anchor polymer-coated units with masonry clips that are screwed to the jambs and to the interior framing members (page 51).

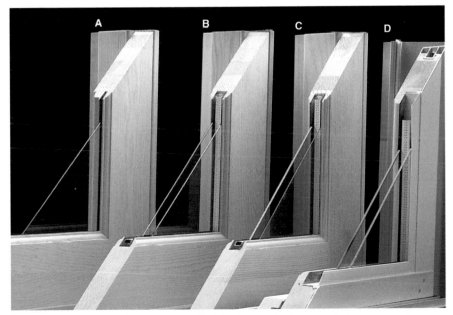 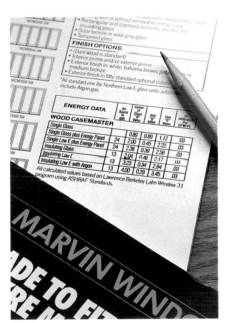

Several types of glass are available from window and door manufacturers. Single-pane glass (A) is suitable only in very mild climates. Double-pane (B) have a sealed air space between the layers of glass to reduce heat loss. They are available in several variations with improved insulating ability, including "low-E" glass with an invisible coating of metal on one surface, and gas-filled windows containing an inert gas, like argon. In southern climates, double-glazed tinted glass (C) reduces heat buildup. Tempered glass (D) has extra strength for use in patio doors and large picture windows.

R-values of windows and doors, listed in manufacturers' catalogs, indicate the energy efficiency of the unit. Higher R-values indicate better insulating properties. Top-quality windows can have an R-value as high as 4.0. Exterior doors with R-values above 10 are considered energy-efficient.

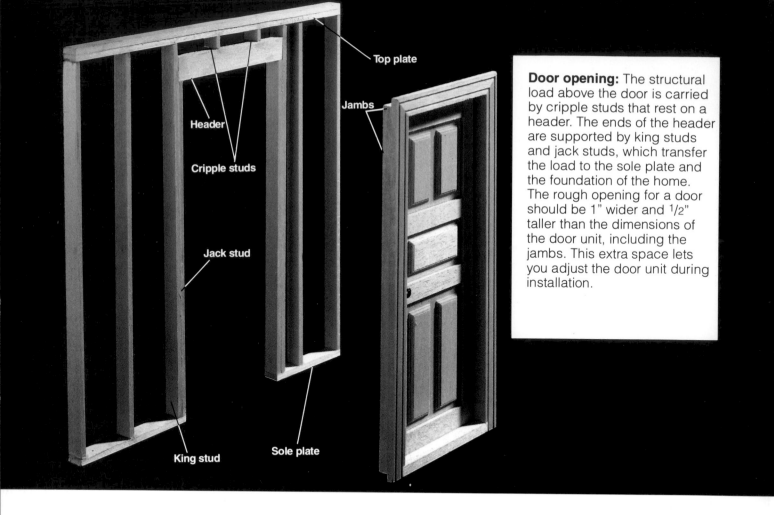

Top plate

Header

Cripple studs

Jambs

Jack stud

King stud

Sole plate

Door opening: The structural load above the door is carried by cripple studs that rest on a header. The ends of the header are supported by king studs and jack studs, which transfer the load to the sole plate and the foundation of the home. The rough opening for a door should be 1" wider and 1/2" taller than the dimensions of the door unit, including the jambs. This extra space lets you adjust the door unit during installation.

Anatomy of Window & Door Openings

Installing new doors or windows often requires cutting one or more studs in a load-bearing wall to create an opening. Remember that the wall openings will require a permanent support beam, called a header, to carry the structural load directly above the removed studs.

The required size for the header is set by the Building Code, and varies according to the width of the rough opening. For a window or door opening, a header can be built from two pieces of 2" dimension lumber sandwiched around ⅜" plywood (chart, right).

If you will be cutting more than one wall stud, make a temporary support to carry the structural load until the header is installed. This support (a top plate and two posts) is held against the ceiling perpendicular to the ceiling joists by hydraulic jacks. Nail together two 2 × 4s that are 4' wider than the rough opening for the top plate. For each post, nail together two 2 × 4s that are 4" shorter than the distance between the ceiling and the top of the jacks. Attach posts to the top plate. Set the support structure onto the jacks and raise until snug against the ceiling.

Recommended Header Sizes

Rough Opening Width	Recommended Header Construction
Up to 3 ft.	⅜" plywood between two 2 x 4s
3 ft. to 5 ft.	⅜" plywood between two 2 x 6s
5 ft. to 7 ft.	⅜" plywood between two 2 x 8s
7 ft. to 8 ft.	⅜" plywood between two 2 x 10s

Recommended header sizes shown above are suitable for projects where a full story and roof are located above the rough opening. This chart is intended for rough estimating purposes only. For actual requirements, contact an architect or your local building inspector. For spans greater than 8 ft., consult a professional.

Window opening: The structural load above the window is carried by cripple studs resting on a header. The ends of the header are supported by king studs and jack studs, which transfer the load to the sole plate and the foundation of the home. The rough sill, which helps anchor the window unit but carries no structural weight, is supported by cripple studs. To provide room for adjustments during installation, the rough opening for a window should be 1" wider and 1/2" taller than the window unit, including the jambs.

Header

Jambs

Jack stud

Top plate

Rough sill

King stud

Cripple stud

Sole plate

Framing Options for Window & Door Openings (new lumber shown in yellow)

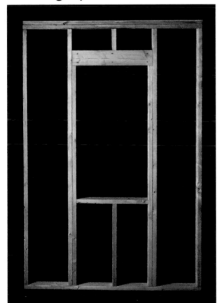

Use an existing opening to avoid new framing work. This is a good option in homes with masonry exteriors, which are difficult to alter. Order a replacement unit that is 1" narrower and 1/2" shorter than the rough opening.

Enlarge an existing opening to simplify the framing work. In many cases you can use an existing king stud and jack stud to form one side of the enlarged opening.

Frame a new opening when installing a window or door where none existed, or when replacing a smaller unit with one that is much larger.

Top plate

Cripple stud

Door header

King stud

Jack stud

Sole plate

Framing & Installing Doors

Your local home center carries many interior and exterior doors in stock sizes. Custom sizes need to be special-ordered, and generally take three or four weeks for delivery.

For easy installation, buy "prehung" interior and exterior doors, which are already mounted in their jambs. Installing unmounted doors is a complicated job best left to a professional.

When replacing an existing door, choosing a new unit the same size as the old door makes your work easier, because you can use framing members already in place.

First, buy the prehung door. Most interior doors are 32" wide, but narrower and wider styles are available. Next, calculate the size for the rough opening and install the door framing.

Most prehung doors are 82" high. Allow an extra ⅜" for clearance, so the unit can be adjusted for plumb and level inside the rough opening. Cut the jack studs 80⅞" long, and set the bottom of the header 82⅜" high. Note: install door (pages 16 to 17) after wallboard is installed.

This section shows:
- Framing a prehung interior door (pages 14 to 15)
- Installing a prehung interior door (pages 16 to 17)
- Cutting off an interior door (pages 18 to 19)
- Installing an entry door (pages 20 to 23)
- Installing a patio door (pages 24 to 29)

Before You Start:
Tools & Materials: prehung door unit, tape measure, 2 × 4 lumber, framing square, 8d common nails, metal connectors, handsaw.

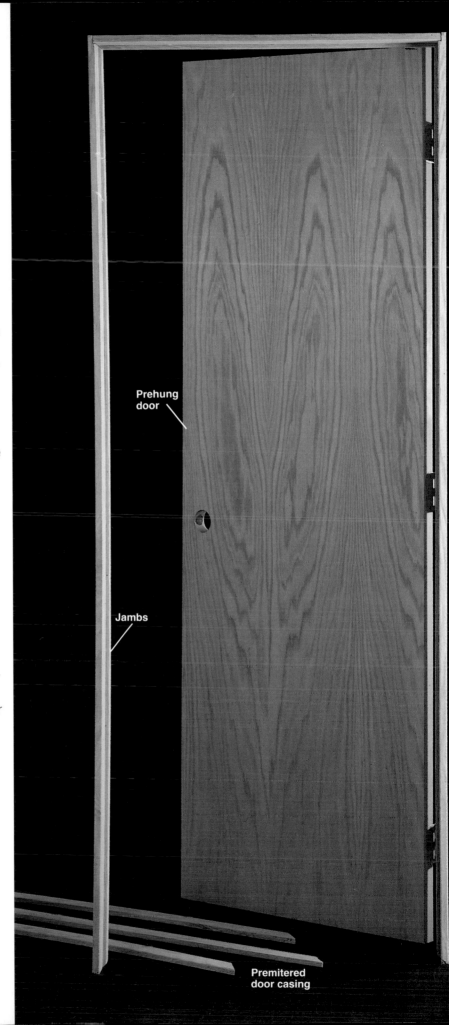

Prehung door

Jambs

Premitered door casing

How to Frame a Prehung Interior Door

King stud marking

King stud marking

Door unit width

Jack stud marking   Extra ⅜"

Extra ⅜"   Jack stud marking

1 Position top of door frame next to top and sole plates, as shown. Measure width of door unit to outside edges of jambs. Mark the distance on top and sole plates. Measure an extra ⅜" on each side and mark plates again. Mark off 1½" stud markings for jack studs and king studs.

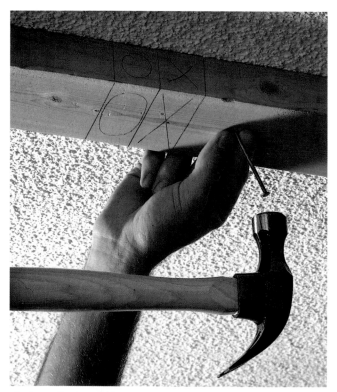

2 Install top plate and sole plate. Do not nail sole plate to floor between jack stud locations, because this portion of plate will be removed before door installation.

King stud

3 Measure and cut king studs and position at markings (X). Drive nails at 45° angle for toenailed joint, or attach studs with metal connectors.

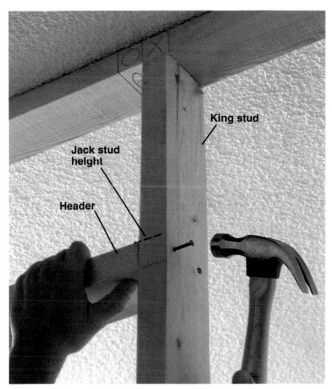

4 Mark height of jack stud on each king stud. Nail header to king stud above 82⅜-inch jack stud mark.

5 Install cripple stud above header, halfway between king studs. Toenail cripple stud to top plate, and nail through bottom of header into cripple stud.

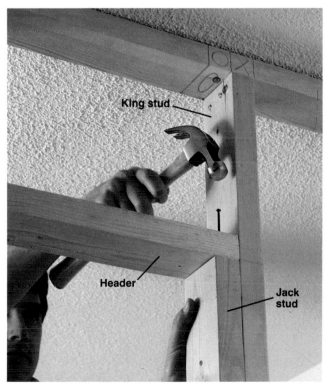

6 Position jack studs against inside of king studs, and nail in place. Nail through top of header down into jack studs.

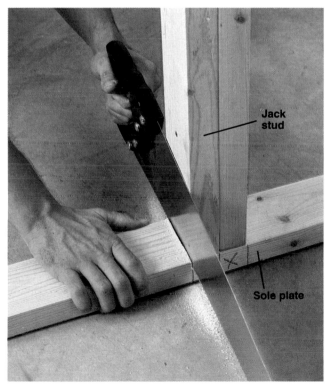

7 Saw through the 2 × 4 sole plate at inside edges of jack studs. Remove cut portion of plate.

15

Installing a Prehung Interior Door

A prehung door unit includes the door, the door jamb, and premitered trim pieces. The hinges are already mortised and attached, and holes are bored for the lock and bolt. The job of installing the door is reduced to two tasks: positioning it plumb and square in the framed opening, and securing it with shims and nails so it swings properly.

Tools & Materials: pry bar, carpenter's level, cedar wood shims, hammer, finish nails (4d and 6d), nail set, saw.

Tip: If unit is to be finished, paint or stain door and trim before installing unit (pages 74 to 76).

How to Install a Prehung Interior Door

1 Remove shipping carton. Inspect unit for damage. Door has casing attached to one side of unit, and is packed with premitered casing for other side of door.

4 Gaps between jamb and framing at hinge and lock locations should be filled with shim material. Nail jamb to frame with 6d finish nails driven through shims.

2 Set door unit into framed opening. Check it for plumb with a carpenter's level.

3 To plumb door unit, insert wood shims between door jamb and frame on hinged side of door. Tap shims with hammer until level shows jamb is plumb.

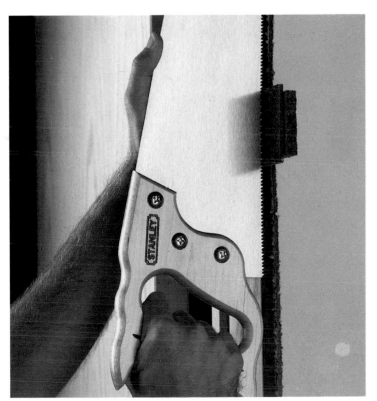

5 Cut off shims with handsaw. Hold saw vertically to avoid damaging the door jamb or wall.

6 Nail premitered trim to jambs, using 4d finish nails driven at 16-inch intervals. Recess nailheads with nail set.

Cutting Off an Interior Door

Prehung interior doors are sized to allow a ¾-inch gap between the bottom of the door and the floor. This gap lets the door swing without binding on the carpet or floorcovering. If thicker carpeting or a larger threshold is installed, a small portion of the door may need to be cut off with a circular saw.

Wider cuts may be needed if a door is altered to fit a special installation, like in a child's room or an undersized storage closet.

Hollow-core interior doors have a solid wood frame, with centers that are hollow. If the entire bottom frame member is cut away when shortening the door, it can be reinserted to close the hollow door cavity.

Before You Start:
Tools & Materials: tape measure, hammer, screwdriver, utility knife, sawhorses, circular saw and straightedge, chisel, carpenter's glue, clamps.

Tip: Measure carefully when marking a door for cutting. Measure from the top of the carpeting, not from the floor.

How to Cut Off an Interior Door

1 With door in place, measure ⅜" up from top of floorcovering and mark door. Remove door from the hinges by removing the hinge pins.

2 Mark cutting line. Cut through door veneer with sharp utility knife to prevent it from chipping when the door is sawed.

3 Lay door on sawhorses. Clamp a straightedge to the door as a cutting guide.

4 Saw off bottom of the door. The hollow core of the door may be exposed.

5 To replace a cut-off frame in the bottom of the door, chisel the veneer from both sides of the removed portion.

6 Apply wood glue to cut-off frame. Insert frame into opening, and clamp. Wipe away excess glue and let dry overnight.

Installing an Entry Door

Prehung entry doors come in many styles, but all are installed using the same basic methods. Because entry doors are very heavy—some large units weigh several hundred pounds—make sure you have help before beginning installation.

To speed your work, do the indoor surface removal and framing work in advance. Before installing the door, make sure you have purchased all necessary locksets and hardware. After installation, protect your door against the weather by painting or staining it immediately, and by adding a storm door (pages 34 to 35) as soon as possible.

Everything You Need:

Tools: metal snips, hammer, level, pencil, circular saw, wood chisel, nail set, caulk gun.

Materials: building paper, drip edge, wood shims, fiberglass insulation, 10d casing nails, silicone caulk.

How to Install an Entry Door

1 Remove the door unit from its packing. Do not remove the retaining brackets that hold the door closed. Remove the exterior surface material inside the framed opening.

2 Test-fit the door unit, centering it in the rough opening. Check to make sure door is plumb. If necessary, shim under the lower side jamb until the door is plumb and level.

Brick molding

3 Trace outline of brick molding on siding. NOTE: If you have vinyl or metal siding, enlarge the outline to make room for the extra trim moldings required by these sidings. Remove the door unit after finishing the outline.

4 Cut the siding along the outline, just down to the sheathing, using a circular saw. Stop just short of the corners to prevent damage to the siding that will remain.

5 Finish the cuts at the corners with a sharp wood chisel.

6 Cut 8"-wide strips of building paper and slide them between the siding and sheathing at the top and sides of the opening, to shield framing members from moisture. Bend paper around the framing members and staple it in place.

Drip edge

7 To provide an added moisture barrier, cut a piece of drip edge to fit the width of the rough opening, then slide between the siding and the building paper at the top of the opening. Do not nail the drip edge.

8 Apply several thick beads of silicone caulk to the subfloor at the bottom of the door opening. Also apply silicone caulk over the building paper on the front edges of the jack studs and header.

(continued next page)

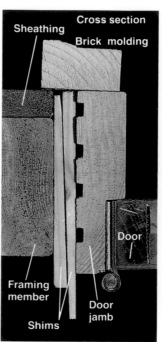

9 Center the door unit in the rough opening, and push the brick molding tight against the sheathing. Have a helper hold the door unit in place until it is nailed in place.

10 From inside, place pairs of hardwood wedge shims together to form flat shims (inset), and insert shims into the gaps between the door jambs and framing members. Insert shims at the lockset and hinge locations, and every 12" thereafter.

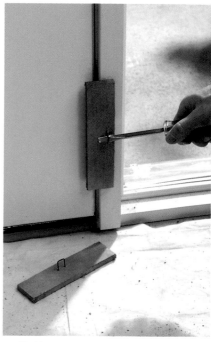

11 Make sure the door unit is plumb. Adjust the shims, if necessary, until the door is plumb and level. Fill the gaps between the jambs and the framing members with loosely packed fiberglass insulation.

12 From outside, drive 10d casing nails through the door jambs and into the framing members at each shim location. Use a nail set to drive the nail heads below the surface of the wood.

13 Remove the retaining brackets installed by the manufacturer, then open and close the door to make sure it works properly.

14 Remove two of the screws on the top hinge and replace them with long anchor screws (usually included with the unit). These anchor screws will penetrate into the framing members to strengthen the installation.

15 Anchor brick molding to the framing members with 10d galvanized casing nails driven every 12". Use a nail set to drive the nail heads below the surface of the wood.

16 Adjust the door threshold to create a tight seal, following manufacturer's recommendations.

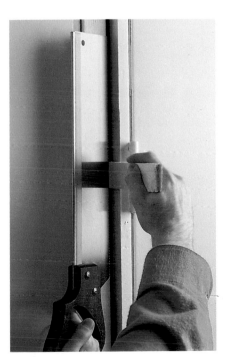

17 Cut off the shims flush with the framing members, using a handsaw.

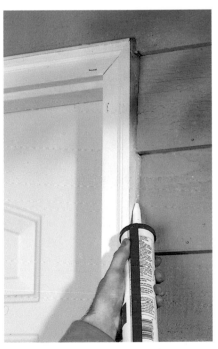

18 Apply silicone caulk around the entire door unit. Fill nail holes with caulk. Finish the door and install the lockset as directed by the manufacturer. See pages 74 to 78 for painting and finishing tips.

Installing a Patio Door

For easy installation, buy a patio door with the door panels already mounted in preassembled frames. Avoid patio doors sold with frame kits that require complicated assembly.

Because patio doors have very long bottom sills and top jambs, they are susceptible to bowing and warping. To avoid these problems, be very careful to install the patio door so it is level and plumb, and to anchor the unit securely to framing members. Yearly caulking and touch-up painting helps prevent moisture from warping the jambs.

Everything You Need:

Tools: pencil, hammer, circular saw, wood chisel, stapler, caulk gun, pry bar, level, cordless screwdriver, handsaw, drill and bits.

Materials: shims, drip edge, building paper, silicone caulk, 10d casing nails, 3" wood screw, sill nosing.

Patio Door Accessory

Screen doors, if not included with the unit, can be ordered from most patio door manufacturers. Screen doors have spring-mounted rollers that fit into a narrow track on the outside of the patio door threshold.

Heavy glass panels may be removed if you must install the door without help. Reinstall the panels after the frame has been placed in the rough opening and nailed at opposite corners. To remove and install the panels, remove the stop rail, found on the top jamb of the door unit.

Adjust the bottom rollers after installation is complete. Remove the coverplate on the adjusting screw, found on the inside edge of the bottom rail. Turn the screw in small increments until the door rolls smoothly along the track without binding when it is opened and closed.

Tips for Installing French-style Patio Doors

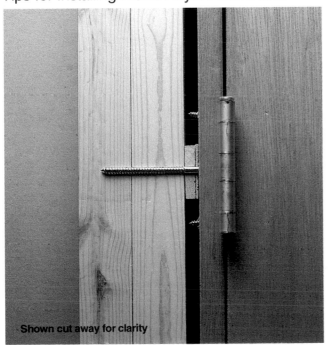

Shown cut away for clarity

Provide extra support for door hinges by replacing the center mounting screw on each hinge with a 3" wood screw. These long screws extend through the side jambs and deep into the framing members.

Keep a uniform 1/8" gap between the door and the side jambs and top jamb to ensure that the door will swing freely without binding. Check this gap frequently as you shim around the door unit.

How to Install a Patio Door

1 Prepare the work area and remove the interior surfaces, then frame the rough opening for the patio door (pages 14 to 15 for framing door openings, pages 45 to 47 for framing openings in exterior walls).

2 Test-fit the door unit, centering it in the rough opening. Check to make sure door is plumb. If necessary, shim under the lower side jamb until the door is plumb and level. Have a helper hold the door in place while it is unattached.

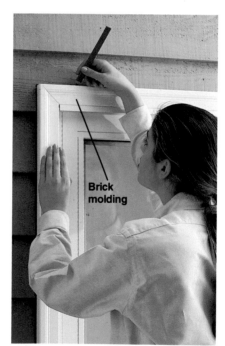

3 Trace the outline of the brick molding onto the siding, then remove the door unit. NOTE: If you have vinyl or metal siding, enlarge the outline to make room for the extra trim moldings required by these sidings.

Brick molding

4 Cut the siding along the outline, just down to the sheathing, using a circular saw. Stop just short of the corners to prevent damage to the siding that will remain. Finish the cuts at the corners with a sharp wood chisel.

Drip edge

5 To provide an added moisture barrier, cut a piece of drip edge to fit the width of the rough opening, then slide it between the siding and the existing building paper at the top of the opening. Do not nail the drip edge.

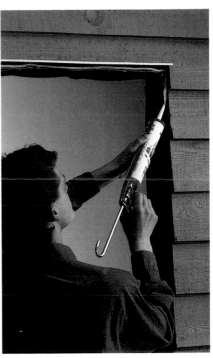

6 Cut 8"-wide strips of building paper and slide them between the siding and the sheathing. Bend the paper around the framing members and staple it in place.

7 Apply several thick beads of silicone caulk to the subfloor at the bottom of the door opening.

8 Apply silicone caulk around the front edge of the framing members, where the siding meets the building paper.

9 Center the patio door unit in the rough opening so the brick molding is tight against the sheathing. Have a helper hold the door unit from outside until it is shimmed and nailed in place.

10 Check the door threshold to make sure it is level. If necessary, shim under the lower side jamb until the patio door unit is level.

(continued next page)

11 If there are gaps between the threshold and subfloor, insert shims coated with caulk into the gaps, spaced every 6". Shims should be snug, but not so tight that they cause the threshold to bow. Clear off excess caulk immediately.

12 Place pairs of hardwood wedge shims together to form flat shims. Insert the shims into the gaps between the side jambs and the jack studs, spaced every 12". For sliding doors, shim behind the strike plate for the door latch.

13 Insert shims into the gap between the top jamb and the header, spaced every 12".

14 From outside, drive 10d casing nails, spaced every 12", through the brick molding and into the framing members. Use a nail set to drive the nail heads below the surface of the wood.

15 From inside, drive 10d casing nails through the door jambs and into the framing members at each shim location. Use a nail set to drive the nail heads below the surface of the wood.

16 Remove one of the screws on the stop block found in the center of the threshold. Replace the screw with a 3" wood screw driven into the subfloor as an anchor.

17 Cut off the shims flush with the face of the framing members, using a handsaw. Fill gaps around the door jambs and beneath the threshold with loosely packed fiberglass insulation.

18 Reinforce and seal the edge of the threshold by installing sill nosing under the threshold and against the wall. Drill pilot holes and attach the sill nosing with 10d casing nails.

19 Make sure the drip edge is tight against the top brick molding, then apply silicone caulk along the top of the drip edge and along the outside edge of the side brick moldings. Fill all exterior nail holes with silicone caulk.

20 Caulk completely around the sill nosing, using your finger to press the caulk into cracks. As soon as the caulk is dry, paint the sill nosing. Finish the door and install the lockset as directed by the manufacturer.

Weatherizing Doors

Door weatherstripping is prone to failure because it undergoes constant stress. Use metal weatherstripping that is tacked to the surfaces whenever you can—especially around door jambs. It is much more durable than self-adhesive products. If your job calls for flexible weatherstripping, use products made from neoprene rubber, not foam. Replace old door thresholds or threshold inserts as soon as they begin to show wear.

Everything You Need:

Tools: putty knife, tack hammer, screwdriver, backsaw, flat pry bar, chisel and mallet, tape measure, drill.

Materials: metal v-channel or tension strips, reinforced felt strips, door sweep, nails or brads, wood filler, caulk, threshold and insert.

The primary heat loss areas in doors (shown highlighted) are around jambs and at the threshold. Install weatherstripping on jambs, and update the threshold and threshold insert to cut down on drafts.

Tips for Weatherizing Doors

Install a storm door to decrease drafts and energy loss through entry doors. Buy an insulated storm door with a continuous hinge and seamless exterior surface.

Adjust the door frame to eliminate large gaps between the door and the jamb. Remove the interior case molding and drive new shims between the jamb and the framing member on the hinge side. Close the door to test the fit, and adjust as needed before reattaching case molding. For added home security, install plywood spacers between shims.

How to Weatherize an Exterior Door

1 Cut two pieces of metal tension strip or v-channel the full height of the door opening, and cut another to full width. Use wire brads to tack the strips to the door jambs and door header, on the interior side of the door stops. TIP: Attach metal weatherstripping from the top down to help prevent buckling. Flare out the tension strips with a putty knife to fill the gaps between the jambs and the door when the door is in closed position (do not pry too far at one time).

2 Add reinforced felt strips to the edge of the door stop, on the exterior side. The felt edge should form a close seal with the door when closed. TIP: Drive fasteners only until they are flush with the surface of the reinforcing spine—overdriving will cause damage and buckling.

3 Attach a new door sweep to the bottom of the door, on the interior side (felt or bristle types are better choices if the floor in your entry area is uneven). Before fastening it permanently, tack the sweep in place and test the door swing to make sure there is enough clearance.

TIP: Fix any cracks in wooden door panels with epoxy wood filler or caulk to block air leaks. If the door has a stain finish, use tinted wood putty, filling from the interior side. Sand down and touch up with paint or stain.

How to Replace a Door Threshold

1 Cut the old threshold in two, using a backsaw. Pry out the pieces, and clean the debris from the sill area below the threshold. Note which edge of the threshold is more steeply beveled; the new threshold should be installed in the same way.

2 Measure the opening for the new threshold, and trim it to fit, using the pieces of the old threshold as templates, if possible. If the profile of the new threshold differs from the old threshold, trace the new profile onto the bottoms of the door stops. Chisel the stops to fit.

3 Apply caulk to the sill. Position the new threshold, pressing it into the caulk. Drive the screws provided with the threshold through the pre-drilled holes in the center channel, and into the sill. Install the threshold insert (see manufacturer's directions).

Tips for Weatherizing Doors

Patio door: Use rubber compression strips to seal the channels in patio door jambs, where movable panels fit when closed. Also install a patio door insulator kit (plastic sheeting installed similarly to plastic sheeting for windows—page 63) on the interior side of the door.

Garage door: Attach a new rubber sweep to the bottom, outside edge of the garage door if the old sweep has deteriorated. Also check the door jambs for drafts, and add weatherstripping, if needed.

How to Secure a Door Frame

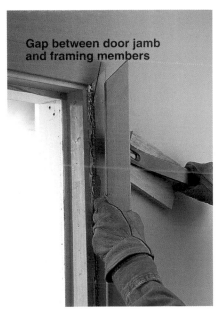

1 Test the frame to find out if it needs shoring up—a loose door frame is much easier for an intruder to pry open. To test the frame, cut a 2 × 4 about 1" longer than the door width. Wedge the board between the jambs, near the lockset. If the frame flexes more than about ¼", proceed to step 2.

2 Remove the interior jamb casing so you can inspect the shims between the jambs and the framing members. Measure the gap, then cut plywood shims from material the same thickness as the gaps. Insert the plywood between the existing shims.

3 Drive 10d casing nails through the jambs and shims, and into the framing members. Set the nail heads, and reattach the casing.

Tips for Securing Doors

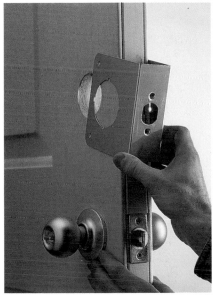

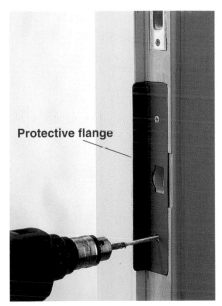

Add metal sleeves to door edges around locksets and deadbolts to help prevent door kick-ins. Make sure the sleeves are the correct thickness for your door.

Add heavy-duty strike plates to reinforce your door and locks, and to help defeat kick-ins, jimmying, and prying. Some strike plates also have a flange that protects the lockset from jimmying and prying.

Install a wide-angle viewer in entry doors to allow you to see outside. Drill an eye-level hole the same diameter as the shaft of the viewer through the door. Insert the shaft so the attached eyepiece is flush against the door. Screw the exterior eyepiece onto the shaft.

Installing a Storm Door

Install a storm door to improve the appearance and weather-resistance of an old entry door, or to protect a newly installed door against weathering. In all climates, adding a storm door can extend the life of an entry door by years.

When buying a storm door, look for models that have a solid inner core and seamless outer shell construction. Carefully note the dimensions of your door opening, measuring from the inside edges of the entry door's brick molding. Choose a storm door that opens from the same side as your entry door.

Adjustable sweeps help make storm doors weathertight. Before installing the door, attach the sweep to the bottom of the door. After the door is mounted, adjust the height of the sweep so it brushes the top of the sill lightly when the door is closed.

Everything You Need:

Tools: tape measure, pencil, plumb bob, hacksaw, hammer, drill and bits, screwdrivers.

Materials: storm door unit, wood spacer strips, 4d casing nails.

How To Cut a Storm Door Frame to Fit a Door Opening

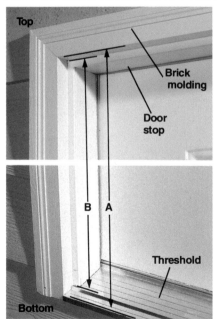

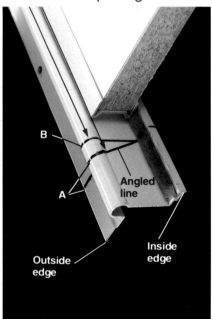

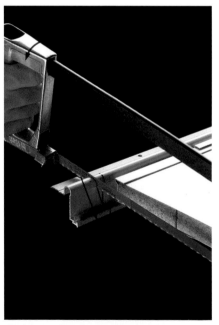

1 Because entry door thresholds are slanted, the bottom of the storm door frame needs to be cut to match the threshold angle. First, measure from the threshold to the top of the door opening along the corner of the brick molding (A), and along the front edge of entry door stop (B).

2 Subtract 1/8" from measurements A and B to allow for small adjustments when the door is installed. Measuring from the top of the storm door frame, mark adjusted points A and B on the corner bead. Draw a line from point A to outside edge of frame and from point B to inside edge. Draw an angled line from point A on corner bead to point B on the inside edge.

3 Use a hacksaw to cut down through the bottom of the storm door frame, following the angled line. Make sure to hold the hacksaw at the same slant as the angled line to ensure that the the cut will be smooth and straight.

How to Fit & Install a Storm Door

Brick molding

Pull tight

1 Position the storm door in the opening and pull the frame tight against the brick molding on the hinge side of the storm door, then draw a reference line onto the brick molding, following the edge of the storm door frame.

Push

2 Push the storm door tight against the brick molding on the latch side, then measure the gap between the reference line and the hinge side of the door frame. If the distance is greater than 3/8", then spacer strips must be installed to ensure the door will fit snugly.

3 To install spacers, remove the door then nail thin strips of wood to the inside of the brick molding at storm door hinge locations. The thickness of the wood strips should be 1/8" less than the gap measured in step 5.

4 Replace the storm door and push it tightly against the brick molding on the hinge side. Drill pilot holes through the hinge side frame of the storm door and into the brick molding, then attach the frame with mounting screws spaced every 12".

5 Remove any spacer clips holding the frame to the storm door. With the storm door closed, drill pilot holes and attach the latch side frame to the brick molding. Use a coin to keep an even gap between the storm door and the storm door frame.

6 Center the top piece of the storm door frame on top of the frame sides. Drill pilot holes and screw the top piece to the brick molding. Adjust the bottom sweep, then attach locks and latch hardware as directed by the manufacturer.

Installing a Security Lock

Security locks have long bolts that extend into the door jamb. They are also called deadbolts. The bolt of a security lock is moved in and out by a keyed mechanism.

Security locks help stop possible break-ins. Often home insurance rates can be lowered with the installation of security locks on exterior doors.

Before You Start:
Tools & Materials: tape measure, security lock (deadbolt), lockset drill kit (including hole saw and spade bit), drill, chisel.

Tip: A double-cylinder deadbolt lock has a key on both sides, and is the best choice for doors that have windows. Knob-type deadbolts can be opened by reaching through broken glass.

How to Install a Security Lock

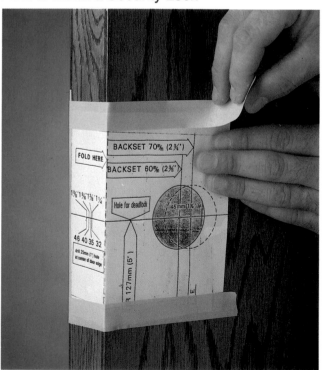

1 Measure to find lock location. Tape cardboard template, supplied with lockset, onto door. Use a nail or awl to mark centerpoints of cylinder and latchbolt holes on door.

2 Bore cylinder hole with a hole saw and drill. To avoid splintering door, drill through one side until hole saw pilot (mandrel) just comes out other side. Remove hole saw, then complete hole from opposite side of door.

3 Use a spade bit and drill to bore latchbolt hole from edge of door into the cylinder hole. Make sure to keep drill perpendicular to door edge while drilling.

4 Insert latchbolt into edge hole. Insert lock tailpiece and connecting screws through the latchbolt mechanism, and screw the cylinders together. Close door to find point where latchbolt meets door jamb.

5 Cut a mortise for strike plate with a chisel. Bore latchbolt hole in center of mortise with spade bit. Install strike plate, using retainer screws provided with lockset.

Repairing a Lockset

How to Clean & Lubricate Locksets

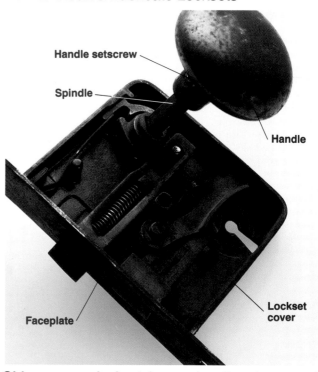

Handle setscrew

Spindle

Handle

Faceplate

Lockset cover

Most lockset problems are solved by cleaning away dirt buildup, then lubricating the inner parts with an all-purpose solvent/lubricant.

When a door will not latch even though the lockset is working smoothly, look for problems with the wood, hinges, strike plate or frame (pages 40 to 43).

Older passage lockset. Loosen handle setscrew and remove handles and attached spindle. Loosen faceplate screws and pry lockset from door. Remove lockset cover or faceplate. Spray solvent/lubricant on all parts. Wipe away the excess lubricant and reassemble lockset.

Before You Start:

Tools & Materials: screwdriver, spray solvent/lubricant.

Tip: If the handle on an older passage lock falls off the spindle, rotate handle to different position on spindle, and retighten setscrew.

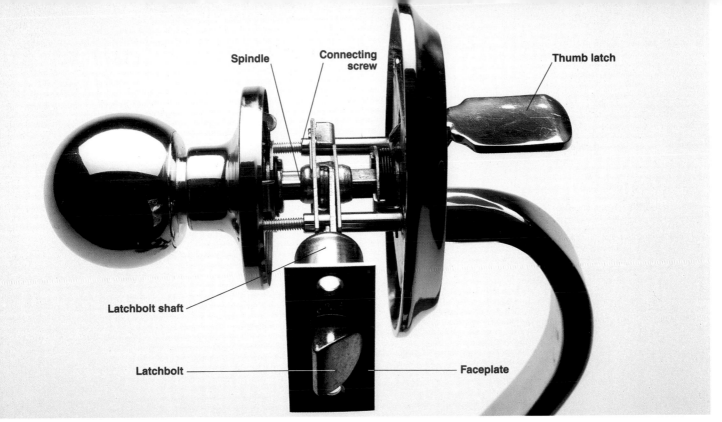

Spindle

Connecting screw

Thumb latch

Latchbolt shaft

Latchbolt

Faceplate

Locksets operate by extending a **latchbolt** through a **faceplate** into a strike plate set into the doorframe. The latchbolt is moved back and forth by a **spindle** or connecting rod operated by a **thumb latch, handle,** or a keyed cylinder.

If a doorknob or key binds when turned, the problem usually lies in the **spindle and latchbolt mechanism.** Cleaning and lubricating the moving parts will correct most problems.

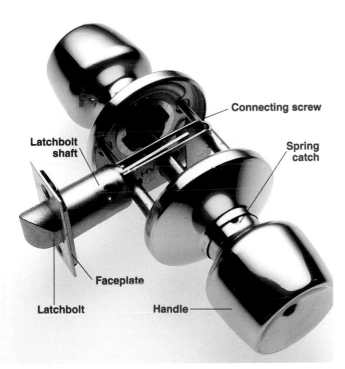

Connecting screw

Latchbolt shaft

Spring catch

Faceplate

Latchbolt

Handle

Modern passage lockset. Remove the handles (held by connecting screws or spring catch). Loosen the retaining screws to remove the faceplate and latchbolt shaft. Spray solvent/lubricant on all parts. Wipe away the excess lubricant and reassemble lockset.

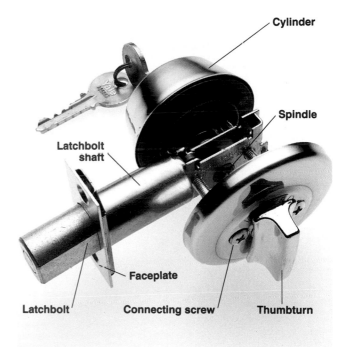

Cylinder

Spindle

Latchbolt shaft

Faceplate

Latchbolt

Connecting screw

Thumbturn

Security locks. Loosen connecting screws to remove inside and outside cylinders. Loosen retaining screws to remove faceplate and latchbolt shaft. Spray solvent/lubricant on all parts. Wipe away the excess lubricant and reassemble lockset.

Sticking latchbolt is caused by dirt and lack of lubrication. Clean and lubricate lockset (pages 39 to 40). Make sure connecting screws on lockset are not too tight. An overly tightened screw will cause latchbolt to bind.

Door Latch Repairs

Latching problems occur when the **latchbolt** binds within the **faceplate**, or when the latchbolt does not slide smoothly into the strike plate opening.

First, make sure the lockset is clean and lubricated (page 39). If latching problems continue, align the latchbolt and strike plate.

Before You Start:

Tools & Materials: metal file, cardboard shims, weights, wood sealer.

Tip: If a latchbolt and strike plate are badly out of alignment, check for problems with the hinges (pages 42 to 43).

Common Causes of Door Latch Problems

Misalignment with strike plate prevents latchbolt from extending into strike plate opening. First, check for loose hinges (page 43). To align strike plate and latchbolt, see opposite page.

Warped door caused by humidity or water penetration can cause latching problems. Check for warping with a straightedge. To straighten a warped door, see opposite page.

How to Align Latchbolt & Strike Plate

1 Fix any loose hinges (page 43) and test door. Fix minor alignment problems by filing the strike plate until the latchbolt fits.

2 Check the door for square fit. If the door is badly tilted, then remove the door (page 42) and shim the top or bottom hinge (right).

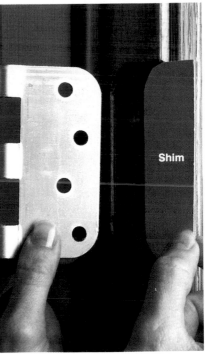

Shim

3 Raise position of latchbolt by inserting thin cardboard shim behind bottom hinge. To lower latchbolt, shim behind top hinge.

How to Straighten a Warped Door

1 Remove door (page 42). Support both ends of warped door on sawhorses. Place heavy weights on bowed center. Leave door weighted for several days until the bow is straightened. Check door with straightedge (page opposite).

2 Apply clear sealer to the ends and edges of door to prevent moisture from entering wood in the future. Rehang the door.

Hinge pin

Freeing a Sticking Door

Doors stick when the hinges sag, or when the wood of the door or door frame swells or shifts.

Make sure the door hinge screws are tight. If a door continues to stick after you tighten the hinges, wait for dry weather to sand or plane the door. If the sticking problem occurs only during unusually wet weather, wait for a dry period, then seal the door edges. This should solve occasional sticking problems.

How to Remove a Door

1 Drive the lower hinge pin out with a screwdriver and hammer. Have a helper hold door in place. Drive out the upper hinge pin.

2 Remove the door and set it aside. Before replacing the door, clean and lubricate all the hinge pins.

How to Tighten Loose Hinges

1 Remove door from hinges (page opposite). Tighten any loose screws. If wood behind hinge will not hold screws, remove hinges.

2 Coat wooden golf tees or dowels with glue and drive them into worn screw holes. Let glue dry. Cut off excess wood.

3 Drill pilot holes in new wood. Rehang hinge with new wood as base for screws.

How to Fix a Sticking Door

1 Tighten any loose hinges (above). If sticking problem continues, use light pencil lines to mark areas where the door sticks.

2 During dry weather, remove door (page opposite). Sand or plane marked areas until door fits. Seal ends and edges with clear wood sealer before rehanging door.

Header

Angled
stud

Shims

Jambs

Double
rough
sill

Insulation

Jack stud

Cripple studs

King stud

Framing & Installing Windows

Most good windows must be custom-ordered several weeks in advance. To save time, do the interior framing work before the window unit arrives. But never open the outside wall surface until you have the window and accessories, and are ready to install them.

Follow the manufacturer's specifications for rough opening size when framing for a window. The listed opening usually is 1" wider and ½" higher than the actual dimension of the window unit.

This section shows:
• Framing a window opening
  (pages 45 to 47)
• Installing a window
  (pages 48 to 51)
• Installing a bay window
  (pages 52 to 61)

The following pages show techniques for wood-frame houses with siding. If you have masonry walls, or if you are installing polymer-coated windows, you may want to attach your window using masonry clips instead of nails (page 51).

Everything You Need:

Tools: tape measure, pencil, combination square, hammer, level, circular saw, handsaw, pry bar, nippers, drill and bits, reciprocating saw, stapler, nail set, caulk gun.

Materials: 10d nails, 2" dimension lumber, 3/8" plywood, shims, building paper, drip edge, casing nails (16d, 8d), fiberglass insulation, silicone caulk.

How to Frame a Window Opening

1 Prepare the project site and remove the interior wall surfaces. Measure and mark rough opening width on sole plate. Mark the locations of the jack studs and king studs on sole plate. Where practical, use existing studs as king studs.

2 Measure and cut king studs, as needed, to fit between the sole plate and top plate. Position the king studs and toenail them to the sole plate with 10d nails.

3 Check the king studs with a level to make sure they are plumb, then toenail them to the top plate with 10d nails.

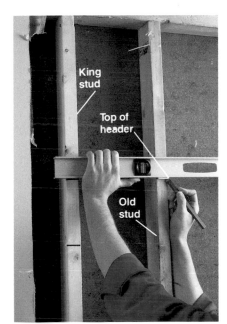

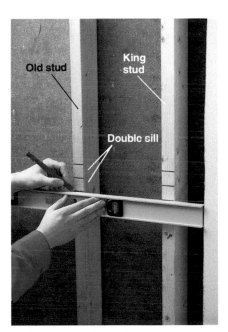

4 Measuring from the floor, mark the rough opening height on one of the king studs. For most windows, the recommended rough opening is 1/2" taller than the height of the window frame. This line marks the bottom of the window header.

5 Measure and mark where the top of the window header will fit against the king stud. The header size depends on the distance between the king studs (page 10). Use a carpenter's level to extend the lines across the old studs to the opposite king stud.

6 Measure down from header line and outline the double rough sill on the king stud. Use a carpenter's level to extend the lines across the old studs to the opposite king stud. **Make temporary supports** (page 10) if you will be removing more than one stud.

(continued next page)

How to Frame a Window Opening (continued)

Bottom of sill

7 Use a circular saw set to maximum blade depth to cut through the old studs along the lines marking the bottom of the rough sill, and along the lines marking the top of the header. Do not cut the king studs. On each stud, make an additional cut about 3" above the first cut. Finish the cuts with a handsaw.

Top of header

Cripple studs

Bottom of sill

8 Knock out the 3" stud sections, then tear out the old studs inside the rough opening, using a pry bar. Clip away any exposed nails, using a nippers. The remaining sections of the cut studs will serve as cripple studs for the window.

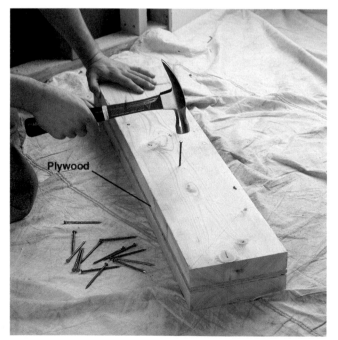

Plywood

9 Build a header to fit between the king studs on top of the jack studs, using two pieces of 2" dimension lumber sandwiched around 3/8" plywood.

10 Cut two jack studs to reach from the top of the sole plate to the bottom header lines on the king studs. Nail the jack studs to the king studs with 10d nails driven every 12". NOTE: On a balloon-frame house the jack studs will reach to the sill plate, or only to the subfloor, if you working on the second story.

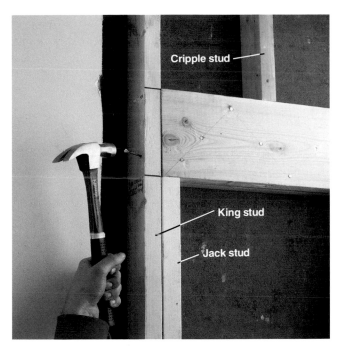

11 Position the header on the jack studs, using a hammer if necessary. Attach the header to the king studs, jack studs, and cripple studs, using 10d nails.

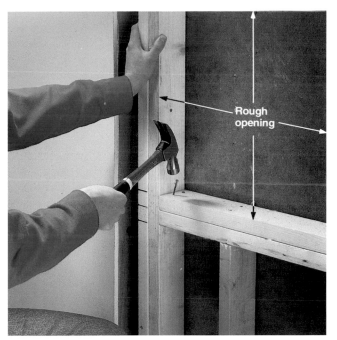

12 Build the rough sill to reach between the jack studs by nailing a pair of 2 × 4s together. Position the rough sill on the cripple studs, and nail it to the jack studs and cripple studs with 10d nails.

Variations for Round-top Windows

Create a template to help you mark the rough opening on the sheathing. Scribe the outline of the curved frame on cardboard, allowing an extra 1/2" for adjustments within the rough opening. A 1/4" × 1 1/4" metal washer makes a good spacer for scribing the outline. Cut out the template along the scribed line.

Tape the template to the sheathing, with the top flush against the header. Use the template as a guide for attaching diagonal framing members across the top corners of the framed opening. The diagonal members should just touch the template. Outline the template on the sheathing as a guide for cutting the rough opening.

How to Install a Window

1 Remove the exterior wall surface, then test-fit the window, centering it in the rough opening. Support the window with wood blocks and shims placed under the bottom jamb. Check to make sure the window is plumb and level, and adjust the shims, if necessary.

2 Trace the outline of the brick molding on the siding. NOTE: if you have vinyl or metal siding, enlarge the outline to make room for the extra J-channel moldings required by these sidings (page 77). Remove the window after finishing the outline.

3 Cut the siding along the outline just down to the sheathing. For a round-top window, use a reciprocating saw held at a shallow angle. For straight cuts, you can use a circular saw adjusted so blade depth equals the thickness of the siding, then use a sharp chisel to complete the cuts at the corners (page 21).

4 Cut 8"-wide strips of building paper and slide them between the siding and sheathing around the entire window opening. Bend the paper around the framing members and staple it in place.

5 Cut a length of drip edge to fit over the top of the window, then slide it between the siding and building paper. For round-top windows, use flexible vinyl drip edge; for rectangular windows, use rigid metal drip edge (inset).

6 Insert the window in the opening, and push the brick molding tight against the sheathing.

7 Check to make sure the window is level.

8 If the window is perfectly level, nail both bottom corners of the brick molding with 10d casing nails. If window is not perfectly level, nail only at the higher of the two bottom corners.

9 If necessary, have a helper adjust the shim under the low corner of the window from the inside, until the window is level.

10 From outside, drive 10d casing nails through the brick molding and into the framing members near the remaining corners of the window.

(continued next page)

11 Place pairs of shims together to form flat shims. From inside, insert shims into the gaps between the jambs and framing members, spaced every 12". On round-top windows, also shim between the angled braces and curved jamb.

12 Adjust the shims so they are snug, but not so tight that they cause the jambs to bow. On multiple-unit windows, make sure the shims under the mull posts are tight.

13 Use a straightedge to check the side jambs to make sure they do not bow. Adjust the shims, if necessary, until the jambs are flat. Open and close the window to make sure it works properly.

14 At each shim location, drill a pilot hole, then drive an 8d casing nail through the jamb and shims and into the framing member, being careful not to damage the window. Drive the nail heads below the wood surface with a nail set.

15 Fill the gaps between the window jambs and the framing members with loosely packed fiberglass insulation. Wear work gloves when handling insulation.

Brick
molding

16 Trim the shims flush with the framing members, using a handsaw.

17 From outside, drive 10d galvanized casing nails, spaced every 12", through the brick moldings and into the framing members. Drive all nail heads below the wood surface with a nail set.

18 Apply silicone caulk around the entire window unit. Fill nail holes with caulk. See page 78 to trim the interior of the window.

Installation Variation: Masonry Clips

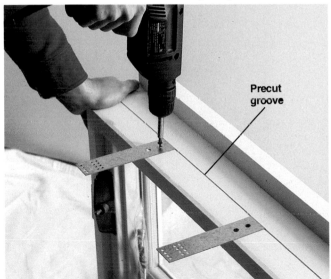

Precut groove

Use metal masonry clips when the brick molding on a window cannot be nailed because it rests against a masonry or brick surface. The masonry clips hook into precut grooves in the window jambs (above, left), and are attached to the jambs with utility screws. After the window unit is positioned in the rough opening, the masonry clips are bent around the framing members and anchored with utility screws (above, right). NOTE: masonry clips also can be used in ordinary lap siding installations if you want to avoid making nail holes in the smooth surface of the brick moldings. For example, windows that are precoated with polymer-based paint can be installed with masonry clips so that the brick moldings are not punctured with nails.

Metal flashing

Roof frame

Sheathing

Shingles

Building paper

Drip edge

Insulation

Cripple stud

Building paper

Header (double 2 × 8s with 3/8" plywood)

Case molding

Preattached head board

Side jamb

Preattached seat board

Support brace

Skirt board

Plastic vapor barrier

Furring strip

Insulation

Siding

Plywood skirt bottom

Rough sill (double 2 × 6s with 3/8" plywood)

Wall sheathing

Cutaway view

Installing a Bay Window

Modern bay windows are pre-assembled for easy installation, but you should still plan on several days to complete the work. Bay windows are large and heavy, and installing them requires special techniques. Have at least one helper to assist you, and try to schedule the work when the chance of rain is small. Use prebuilt bay window accessories (page opposite) to speed your work.

A large bay window can weigh several hundred pounds, so it must be anchored securely to framing members in the wall, and supported by braces attached to framing members below the window. Some window manufacturers include cable-support hardware that can be used instead of metal support braces.

Everything You Need:

Tools: circular saw, caulk gun, hammer, screw gun, framing square, tape measure, level, screwdriver, chisel, stapler, metal snips, roofing knife, T-bevel, utility knife.

Materials: bay window, prebuilt roof skirt, metal support brackets, galvanized utility screws (2", 2 1/2", 3"), building paper, sheet plastic, fiberglass insulation, 2 × 2 lumber, 5 1/2" skirt board, 3/4" exterior-grade plywood, shingles, roofing cement, wood shims, galvanized casing nails (16d, 8d), silicone caulk.

Prebuilt Accessories for Bay Windows

For easy installation, use prebuilt accessories when installing a bay window. Roof frames (A) come complete with sheathing (B), metal top flashing (C) and step flashing (D) and can be special-ordered at home centers that sell bay windows. You will need to specify the exact size of your window unit, and the angle (pitch) you want for the roof. You can cover the roof inexpensively with building paper and shingles, or order a copper or aluminum shell from your home center. Metal support braces (E) and skirt boards (F) can be ordered at your home center if they are not included with the window unit. Use two braces for bay windows up to 5 ft. wide, and three braces for larger windows. Skirt boards are clad with aluminum or vinyl, and can be cut to fit with a circular saw or power miter saw.

Framing a Bay Window

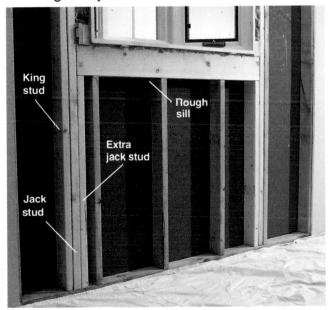

Bay window framing resembles that for a standard window, except that it requires an extra-strong rough sill built from a pair of 2 × 6s sandwiched around a layer of ⅜" plywood (page 46). Because the sill carries considerable weight, extra jack studs are installed under each end of the sill. See pages 44 to 47 for basic window framing techniques.

Roof Framing Variation

Build an enclosure above the bay window if the roof soffit overhangs the window. Build a 2 × 2 frame (top) to match the angles of the bay window, and attach the frame securely to the wall and overhanging soffit. Install a vapor barrier and insulation (page 57), then finish the enclosure so it matches the house siding (bottom).

How to Install a Bay Window

1 Prepare project site and remove interior wall surfaces, then frame the rough opening (pages 45 to 47). Remove exterior wall surface. Mark a section of siding directly below rough opening for removal. Width of marked area should equal that of window unit, and height should equal that of skirt board.

2 Set the blade on a circular saw just deep enough to cut through the siding, then cut along the outline. Stop just short of the corners to avoid damaging the siding outside the outline. Use a sharp chisel to complete the corner cuts (page 21). Remove the cut siding inside the outline.

3 Position the support braces along the rough sill within the widest part of the bay window and above the cripple stud locations. Add cripple studs to match support brace locations if necessary. Draw outlines of the braces on the top of the sill. Use a chisel or circular saw to notch the sill to a depth equal to the thickness of the support braces.

4 Slide the support braces down between the siding and the sheathing. You may need to pry the siding material away from the sheathing slightly to make room for the braces. NOTE: On stucco, you will need to chisel notches in masonry wall surface to fit the support braces.

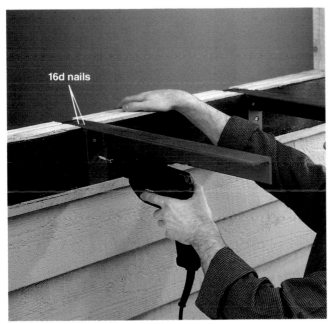

5 Attach the braces to the rough sill with galvanized 16d nails. Drive 3" utility screws through the front of the braces and into the rough sill to prevent twisting.

6 Lift the bay window onto the support braces and slide it into the rough opening. Center the window in the opening.

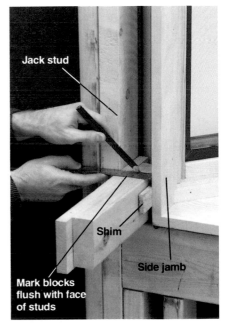

7 Check the window unit to make sure it is level. If necessary, drive shims under the low side to level the window. Temporarily brace the outside bottom edge of the window with 2 × 4s to keep it from moving on the braces.

8 Set the roof frame on top of the window, with sheathing loosely tacked in place. Trace the outline of the window and roof unit onto the siding. Leave a gap of about 1/2" around the roof unit to allow room for the flashing and shingles.

9 Mark and cut wood blocks to bridge the gap between side jambs and studs, if gap is more than 1" wide. (Smaller gaps require no blocks.) Leave a small space for inserting wood shims. Remove the window, then attach blocks every 12" along the studs.

(continued next page)

10 Cut the siding just down to the sheathing along the outline, using a circular saw. Stop just short of corners, then use a wood chisel to complete the corner cuts. Remove cut siding. Pry remaining siding slightly away from the sheathing around the roof outline to allow for easy installation of the metal flashing. Cover the exposed sheathing with 8"-wide strips of building paper (see step 4, page 48).

11 Set the bay window unit back on the braces and slide it back into the rough opening until the brick moldings are tight against the sheathing. Insert wood shims between the outside end of the metal braces and the seat board (inset). Check the window to make sure it is level, and adjust the shims if necessary.

12 Anchor the window by driving 16d galvanized casing nails through the outside brick molding and into the framing members. Space the nails every 12", and use a nail set to drive the nail heads below the surface of the wood.

13 Drive wood shims into the spaces between the side jambs and the blocking or jack studs, and between the headboard and header. Space the shims every 12". Fill the spaces around the window with loosely packed fiberglass insulation. At each shim location, drive 16d casing nails through the jambs and shims and into the framing members. Cut off the shims flush with the framing members, using a handsaw. Use a nail set to drive the nail heads below the surface of the wood.

14 Staple sheet plastic over the top of the window unit to serve as a vapor barrier. Trim the edges of the plastic around the top of the window with a utility knife.

15 Remove the sheathing pieces from the roof frame, then position the frame on top of the window unit. Attach the roof frame to the window and to the wall at stud locations, using 3" utility screws.

16 Fill the empty space inside the roof frame with loosely packed fiberglass insulation. Screw the sheathing back onto the roof frame.

17 Staple asphalt building paper over the roof sheathing. Make sure each piece overlaps the one below by at least 5".

18 Cut drip edges with metal snips, then attach them around the edge of the roof sheathing, using roofing nails.

(continued next page)

19 Cut and fit a piece of step flashing on each side of the roof unit. Adjust the flashing so it overhangs the drip edge by 1/4". Flashings help guard against moisture damage.

20 Trim the end of the flashing to the same angle as the drip edge. Nail flashing to the sheathing with roofing nails.

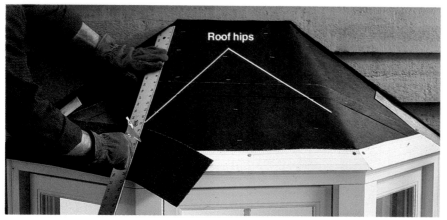

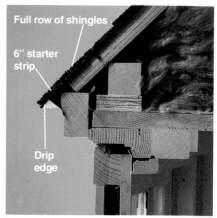

21 Cut a 6"-wide strip of shingles for the starter row. Use roofing nails to attach the starter row so it overhangs the drip edge by about 1/2" (photo, right). Cut the shingles along the roof hips with a straightedge and roofing knife.

22 Nail a full row of shingles over the starter row. Bottom edges should be flush with bottom of the starter row, and notches should not be aligned.

23 Install another piece of step flashing on each side of the roof, overlapping the first piece of flashing by about 5".

24 Cut and install another row of full shingles. Bottom edges should overlap the tops of the notches on previous row by 1/2". Attach the shingles with roofing nails driven just above the notches.

25 Continue installing alternate rows of step flashing and shingles to top of roof. Bend the last pieces of step flashing to fit over the roof hips.

26 When roof sheathing is covered with shingles, install top flashing. Cut and bend the ends over the roof hips, and attach with roofing nails. Attach remaining rows of shingles over the top flashing.

27 Find the height of final rows of shingles by measuring from the top of the roof to a point 1/2" below the top of the notches on the last installed shingle. Trim shingles to this measurement.

28 Attach the final row of shingles with a thick bead of roofing cement, not nails. Press firmly to ensure a good bond.

29 Make ridge caps by cutting shingles into 1-ft. sections. Use a roofing knife to trim off the top corners of each piece, so ridge caps will be narrower at the top than at the bottom.

30 Install the ridge caps over the roof hips, beginning at the bottom of the roof. Trim the bottom ridge caps to match the edges of the roof. Keep the same amount of overlap with each layer.

(continued next page)

31 At the top of the roof hips, use a roofing knife to cut the shingles to fit flush with the wall. Attach the shingles with roofing cement. Do not nail.

32 Staple sheet plastic over the bottom of the window to serve as a vapor barrier. Trim plastic around the bottom of the window with a utility knife.

33 Cut and attach a 2 × 2 skirt frame around the bottom of the bay window, using 3" galvanized utility screws. The skirt frame should be set back about 1" from the edges of the window.

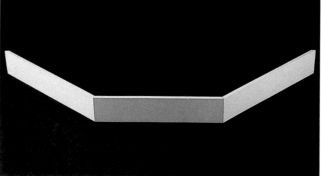

34 Cut skirt boards to match the shape of the bay window bottom, mitering the ends to ensure a tight fit. Test-fit the skirt board pieces to make sure they match the bay window bottom.

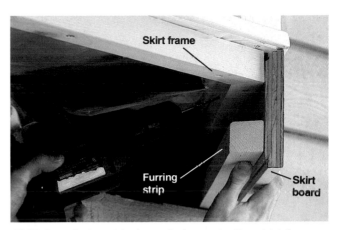

35 Cut a 2 × 2 furring strip for each skirt board. Miter the ends to the same angles as the skirt boards. Attach the furring strips to the back of the skirt boards, 1" from the bottom edges, using 2" galvanized utility screws.

36 Attach the skirt board pieces to the skirt frame. Drill 1/8" pilot holes every 6" through the back of the skirt frame and into the skirt boards, then attach the skirt boards with 2" galvanized utility screws.

37 Measure the space inside the skirt boards, using a T-bevel to duplicate the angles. Cut a skirt bottom from 3/4" exterior-grade plywood to fit this space.

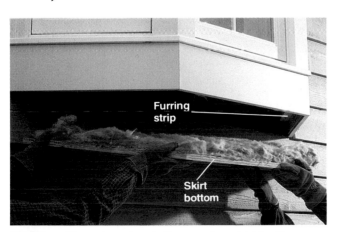

38 Lay fiberglass insulation on the skirt bottom. Position the skirt bottom against the furring strips and attach it by driving 2" galvanized utility screws every 6" through the bottom and into the furring strips.

39 Install any additional trim pieces specified by your window manufacturer (inset), using casing nails. Seal roof edges with roofing cement, and seal around the rest of the window with silicone caulk. Complete the inside finish work (page 78).

The primary heat loss areas in windows (shown highlighted) should be sealed with the appropriate weatherstripping material. This can increase the energy efficiency of a window by 100% or more.

Weatherizing Windows

The secret to energy-tight windows is blocking air movement, creating a sealed-off dead air space between interior and exterior glass panes.

Modern double and triple-paned windows often contain inert gases between panes to help create dead air spaces. You can create dead air spaces in older windows by using weatherstripping and a good storm window (or plastic window sheeting) to block air movement. Weatherstripping the inside gaps helps keep warm, moist air on the interior side of a window, minimizing condensation and frosting between the window and the storm.

Everything You Need:

Tools: tack hammer, aviator snips, putty knife, hair dryer, staple gun.

Materials: metal v-channel, compressible foam, tubular gasket, reinforced felt, brads, clear silicone caulk, siliconized acrylic caulk, peelable caulk, plastic sheeting (interior and exterior).

How to Weatherstrip Windows

1 Cut metal v-channel to fit in the channels for the sliding sash, extending at least 2" past the closed position for each sash (do not cover sash-closing mechanisms). Attach the v-channel by driving wire brads (usually provided by the manufacturer) with a tack hammer. Drive the fasteners flush with the surface so the sliding sash will not catch on them.

2 Flare out the open ends of the v-channels with a putty knife so the channel is slightly wider than the gap between the sash and the track it fits into. Avoid flaring out too much at one time—it is difficult to press v-channel back together without causing buckling.

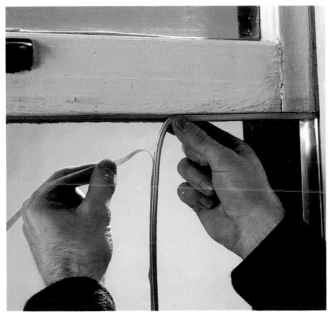

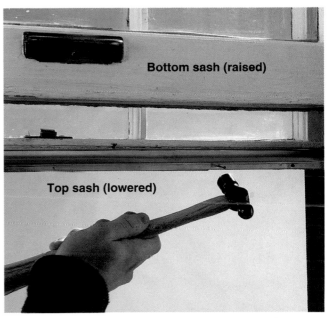

Bottom sash (raised)

Top sash (lowered)

3 Wipe down the underside of the bottom window sash with a damp rag, and let it dry; then, attach self-adhesive compressible foam or rubber to the underside of the sash. Use high-quality hollow neoprene strips, if available. This will create an air-tight seal when the window is locked in position.

4 Seal the gap between the top sash and the bottom sash on double-hung windows. Lift the bottom sash and lower the top sash to improve access, and tack metal v-channel to the bottom rail of the top sash using wire brads. TIP: The open end of the "v" should be pointed downward so moisture cannot collect in the channel. Flare out the v-channel with a putty knife to fit the gap between the sash.

Tips for Weatherizing Windows

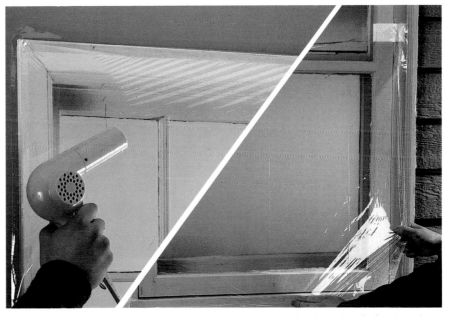

Apply caulk around the interior window casing with clear silicone caulk. For added protection, lock the window in the closed position, and caulk the gaps around the interior edges of the sash with clear, peelable caulk (which can be removed easily when the heating season is over).

Add plastic sheeting or shrink-wrap product to the interior (left photo) to block drafts and keep moisture away from the window surfaces. Follow the manufacturer's installation directions, which often include using a hair dryer to tighten the plastic and remove wrinkles, making it almost invisible. Install exterior plastic sheeting (right photo) on the outside of your window, following the manufacturer's directions (rolls of tacking or stapling strips are often included with the product).

(continued next page)

Tips for Weatherizing Windows (continued)

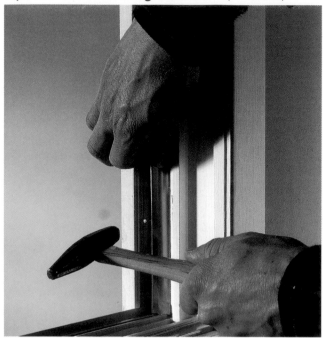

Sliding windows (side by side): Treat side-by-side sliding windows as if they were double-hung windows (pages 62 to 63) turned 90°. For greater durability, substitute metal tension strips for self-adhesive compressible foam in the sash track that fits against the edge of the sash when the window is closed.

Casement windows: Attach self-adhesive foam or rubber compression strips on the outside edges of the window stops.

Tips for Weatherizing Storm Windows

Storm windows: Create a tight seal by attaching foam compression strips to the outside of the storm window stops (left photo). After installing the storm window, fill any gaps between the exterior window trim and the storm window with caulk backer rope. Check the inside surface of the storm window during cold weather for condensation or frost buildup. If moisture is trapped between the storm window and the permanent window, drill one or two small holes through the bottom rail of the storm window (right photo) to allow moist air to escape. Drill at a slight upward angle.

Replacing Storm Windows

As old removable storm windows wear out, many homeowners elect to replace them with modern combination storm windows. Designed to mount permanently in the existing opening, "retrofit" combination storm windows are very easy to install, and fairly inexpensive.

Most retrofit storm windows attach to the outside edges of the window stops on the sides and top of the window opening. Most windows do not have a bottom stop. Secure the bottom rail of the new window with caulk. Common window sizes are stocked at most building centers, but you may need to order custom-made windows. Bring exact measurements (photo, right) when you order the windows. You also will be asked to choose a finish color and a style. If you have operating double-hung windows, choose 3-sash windows so you have the option of opening the top storm sash.

Everything You Need:

Tools: screwdriver, drill, tape measure.

Materials: replacement storm windows, caulk or panel adhesive, screws.

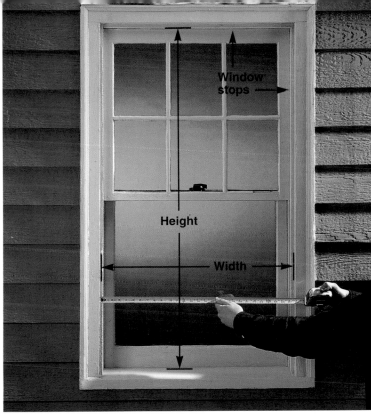

"Retrofit" storm windows attach to the window stops in the existing window opening. The easiest way to size them is to use the dimensions of old storms. Otherwise, measure the narrowest point between side jambs to find the width, and measure the shortest point from the header to the sill (where it meets the front edges of the stops) to find the height.

How to Install New Combination Storm Windows

1 Buy replacement storm windows to fit your window openings (photo, above). Test-fit windows before installing them. To install, first apply a bead of exterior-grade panel adhesive or caulk to the outside edges of the window stops at the top and sides.

2 Predrill pilot holes for fasteners in the mounting flanges, spaced 12" apart, making sure they will be centered over the stops. Press the new storm window into the opening, centered between the side stops, with the bottom rail resting on the window sill.

3 Drive fasteners (#4 × 1" sheet-metal screws work well), starting at the top. Make sure the window is squarely in the opening, then fill in the fasteners on the side stops. Apply caulk along the bottom rail, leaving a ¼"-wide gap midway to function as a weep hole.

Maintaining Storm Doors & Windows

Removable storm windows are excellent insulators when they are in good condition, and removable screens provide full ventilation. For these reasons, many homeowners still prefer them over combination storm and screen windows—even though they must be changed with the seasons.

Simple wood-sash construction and a lack of moving parts make removable storm and screen windows easy to repair and maintain. Replacing screening or glass, tightening loose joints, and applying fresh paint are the primary maintenance jobs.

Combination storm and screen windows offer convenience, and can be repaired simply if you have a little know-how and the right replacement parts.

Build a storage rack for removable screens and storm windows. Simply attach a pair of 2 × 4s to the rafters of your garage or the ceiling joists in your basement. Attach window-hanger hardware to the top rails of the screen and storm windows, if they do not already have them. Space the hangers uniformly. Then, attach screw eyes to the 2 × 4s in matching rows to fit the window hangers.

Tools & Materials

Tools and materials for repairing and maintaining storm windows include: rubber mallet (A), spline cord for metal sash (B), epoxy wood filler (C), penetrating lubricant (D), roof cement (E), siliconized acrylic caulk (F), staple gun (G), epoxy glue (H), brad pusher (I), turnbuttons (J), retaining strips for wood sash (K), metal sash replacement hardware (L), wire brads (M), glazier's points (N), rubber window gasket for metal sash (O), glass cutter (P), putty knife (Q), spline roller (R), tack hammer (S).

Slide tab

Remove metal storm window sash by pressing in the release hardware in the lower rail (like the slide tabs above), then lifting the sash out. Sash hangers on the corners of the top rail (see step 2, next page) should be aligned with the notches in the side channels before removal.

Repairing Metal Storm Windows

Compared to removable wood storm windows, repairing combination storms is a little more complex. But there are several repairs you can make without too much difficulty, as long as you find the right parts. Bring the old corner keys, gaskets, or other original parts to a hardware store that repairs storm windows so the clerk can help you find the correct replacement parts (page 69, step 3). If you cannot find the right parts, have a new sash built.

Everything You Need:

Tools: tape measure, scissors, utility knife, spline roller, drill, screwdriver, hammer, nail set.

Materials: spline cord, rubber gasket, glass, screening, replacement hardware.

How to Replace Screening in a Metal Storm Window

1 Remove the spline cord holding the damaged screening in the frame. Also remove the old screening material, and clean any debris from the spline-cord tracks in the frame.

2 Cut the new screening material at least 3" wider and longer than the frame opening, and lay it over the frame. Set the spline cord over the screening so it is aligned with the spline-cord track.

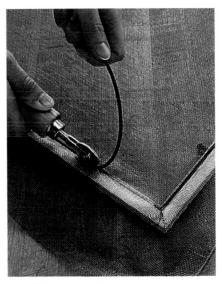

3 At the top of the window, press the spline cord into the spline-cord track with a spline roller. Stretch the screening across the opening and continue setting the cord all the way around the frame. Trim off the excess screening with a utility knife.

How to Replace Glass in a Metal Storm Window

1 Remove the sash frame from the window, then completely remove the broken glass from the sash. Remove the rubber gasket that framed the old glass pane and remove any glass remnants. Find the dimensions for the replacement glass by measuring between the inside edges of the frame opening, then adding twice the thickness of the rubber gasket to each measurement.

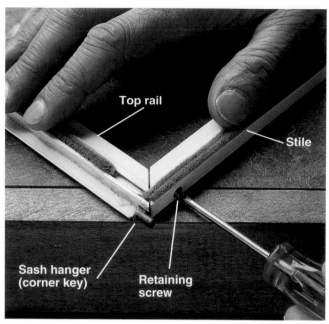

2 Set the frame on a flat surface, and disconnect the top rail. Normally, you need to remove the retaining screws in the sides of the frame stiles where they join the top rail. After unscrewing the retaining screws, pull the top rail loose, pulling gently in a downward motion to avoid damaging the L-shaped corner keys that join the rail and the stiles. For glass replacement, you need only disconnect the top rail.

3 Fit the rubber gasket (buy a replacement if the original is in poor condition) around one edge of the replacement glass pane. At corners, cut the spine of the gasket partway so it will bend around the corner. Continue fitting the gasket around the pane, cutting at the corners, until all four edges are covered. Trim off any excess gasket material.

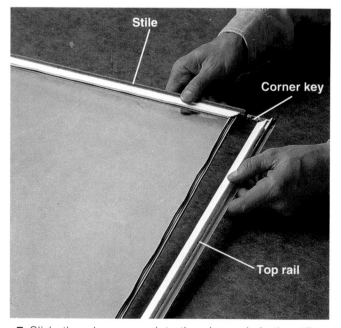

4 Slide the glass pane into the channels in the stiles and the bottom rail of the sash frame. Insert the corner keys into the top rail, then slip the other ends of the keys into the frame stiles. Press down on the top rail until the mitered corners are flush with the stiles. Drive the retaining screws back through the stiles and into the top rail to join the frame together. Insert the frame back into the window.

How to Disassemble & Repair a Metal Sash Frame

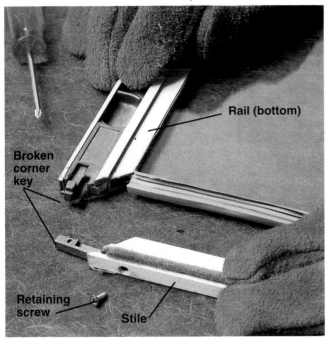

Broken corner key

Rail (bottom)

Retaining screw

Stile

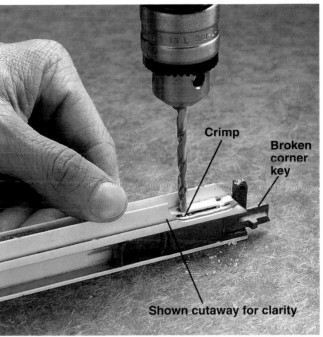

Crimp

Broken corner key

Shown cutaway for clarity

1 Metal window sash are held together at the corner joints by L-shaped pieces of hardware that fit into grooves in the sash frame pieces. To disassemble a broken joint, start by disconnecting the stile and rail at the broken joint—there is usually a retaining screw driven through the stile that must be removed.

2 Corner keys are secured in the rail slots with crimps that are punched into the metal over the key. To remove keys, drill through the metal in the crimped area, using a drill bit the same diameter as the crimp. Carefully knock the broken key pieces from the frame slots with a screwdriver and hammer.

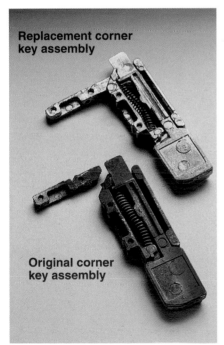

Replacement corner key assembly

Original corner key assembly

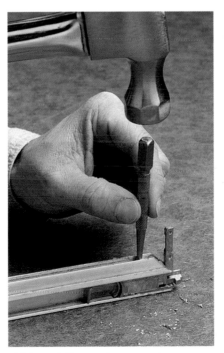

3 Locate matching replacement parts for the broken corner key (page 67), which is usually an assembly of two or three pieces. There are dozens of different types, so it is important that you save the old parts for reference.

4 Insert the replacement corner key assembly into the slot in the rail. Use a nail set as a punch, and rap it into the metal over the corner key, creating a new crimp to hold the key in place.

5 Insert the glass and gasket into the frame slots (see previous page), then reassemble the frame and drive in retainer screws (for screen windows, replace the screening).

Repairing Wood Storm Windows & Screens

Because they are installed, removed, transported, and stored so frequently, removable wood storm windows need repair and maintenance regularly. Broken glass, torn screens, loose joints or hangers, dry or missing glazing, and failed paint are the primary problems. Fortunately, fixing wood storm windows is simple, and maintaining them well has a high payback in the appearance and efficiency of your house.

Everything You Need:

Tools: utility knife, clamps, drill, mallet, putty knife, staple gun, tack hammer, scissors.

Materials: epoxy glue, dowels, caulk, replacement glass, glazier's points, glazing compound, screening, wire brads.

Clean out recesses for glass and screening by carefully removing old glass, glazing compound, and glazier's points (or screening and retaining strips). Scrape residue from the recess with an old chisel, then paint with a coat of primer or sealer before installing new glass or screen.

How to Repair Loose Joints in Wood Sash Frames

1 Remove the glass or screening, then carefully separate the loose joint, using a flat pry bar if necessary. Scrape the mating surfaces clean. Inject epoxy glue into the joint (plain wood glue should not be used for exterior work). Press the mating surfaces back together and clamp with bar clamps, making sure the frame is square.

2 After the glue is dry, reinforce the repair by drilling two ⅜"-diameter holes through the joint (mortise-and-tenon joints are common). Cut two ⅜"-diameter dowels about 1" longer than the thickness of the frame, and round over one end of each dowel with sandpaper. Coat the dowels with epoxy glue, and drive them through the holes. After the glue dries, trim the ends of the dowels with a backsaw, then sand until they are flush with the sash. Touch up with paint.

How to Replace Glass in a Wood Storm Window

1 Clean and prepare the glass recess (top photo, previous page). Measuring from the outside shoulders of the glass recess, measure the full width and height of the opening, subtract ⅛" from each dimension, and have new glass cut to fit. Apply a thin bead of caulk in the recess to create a bed for the new pane of glass.

2 Press the new glass pane into the fresh caulk. Use a putty knife or screwdriver blade to push glazier's points into the frame every 8" to 10" to hold the glass in place.

3 Roll glazing compound into ⅜"-diameter "snakes" and press the snakes into the joint between the glass and the frame. Smooth the compound with a putty knife held at a 45° angle to create a flat surface. Strip off the excess. Let the compound dry for several days before painting.

How to Replace Screening in a Wood Storm Window

1 Completely clean and prepare the recess (top photo, previous page). Cut a new piece of screening at least 3" longer in height and in width than the opening. TIP: Use fiberglass screening for residential windows—it is easy to work with, and will not rust or corrode.

2 Tack the top edge of the screening into the recess with a staple gun. Stretch the screen tightly toward the bottom. Tack the bottom into the recess. Tack one side in place. Then, stretch the screening tightly across the frame, and tack the other side.

3 Attach retaining strips over the edges of the screening. Do not use old nail holes: drill ½"-diameter pilot holes in the retaining strips, then drive 1" wire brads. Trim off excess screening with a sharp utility knife.

Repairing Loose or Sticking Windows

Windows stick because the channels or guides need cleaning and lubricating, or because they have been painted shut.

Loose windows that refuse to stay open may have broken sash cords or chains.

Newer double-hung windows are balanced by springs, and have adjustment screws to control window movement.

Before You Start:

Tools & Materials: paint zipper or utility knife, hammer, screwdriver, small pry bar, sash cord.

Tips for Freeing a Sticking Window

Cut paint film, if window is painted shut. Insert a paint zipper or utility knife into crack between window stop and sash.

Place block of scrap wood along window sash. Tap lightly with a hammer to free window.

How to Adjust Spring-loaded Windows

Adjust screw found on track insert. Turn screw until window is properly balanced.

How to Replace Broken Sash Cords

1 Cut any paint seal between the window frame and stops using a utility knife or paint zipper. Pry stops away from frame with small pry bar, or remove molding screws.

2 Bend stops in a slight curve from center of frame to remove them. Remove any metal weather-stripping by pulling nails holding strips in channel.

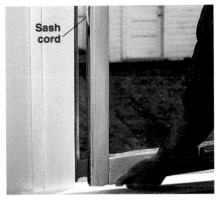

Sash cord

3 Slide out the lower window. Pull knotted or nailed cords from holes in side window sashes.

Weight pocket

4 Pry out or unscrew cover of weight pocket found in lower end of window channel. Reach inside pocket and remove the weight. Remove old sash cord from weight.

Pulley

5 Tie piece of string to small nail. Tie other end of string to new sash cord. Run nail over the pulley wheel and let it drop into weight pocket. Retrieve nail and string through open pocket.

6 Pull on string to run new sash cord over pulley wheel and through weight pocket. Make sure new cord runs smoothly over pulley wheel.

Weight

7 Attach end of new sash cord to the weight using a tight double knot. Return the weight to the open pocket and pull on sash cord to raise weight up against pulley.

8 Rest bottom window on sill. Hold sash cord firmly against side of window, and cut enough cord to measure 3 inches past hole in side window sash.

Sash

Knot

9 Knot sash cord and wedge knot into hole in window sash. Replace the pocket cover. Slide window and weatherstripping back into frame. Nail weatherstripping and replace stops.

Painting Trim

When painting an entire room, paint the wood trim first, then the walls. Start by painting the inside portions of trim and working out toward walls. On windows, for instance, first paint the edges close to the glass, then the surrounding face trim.

Doors should be painted quickly because of the large surface. To avoid lap marks, always paint from dry surfaces back into wet paint. On baseboards, cut in the top edge and work down to the flooring. Plastic floor guards or a wide broadknife can help shield carpet and wood flooring from paint drips.

Alkyds and latex enamels may require two coats. Always sand lightly between coats and wipe with a tack cloth so that the second coat bonds properly.

How to Paint a Window

1 To paint double-hung windows, remove them from frames, if possible. Newer, spring-mounted windows are released by pushing against the frame (arrow).

2 Drill holes and insert 2 nails into the legs of wooden stepladder, and mount the window easel-style for easy painting; or lay window flat on bench or sawhorses. Do not paint sides or bottom of sashes.

3 Using a tapered sash brush, begin by painting the wood next to the glass. Use narrow edge of brush, and overlap paint onto the glass to create a weatherseal.

4 Clean excess paint off glass with a putty knife wrapped in a clean cloth. Rewrap the knife often so that you always wipe with clean fabric. Leave 1/16'' paint overlap from sash onto glass.

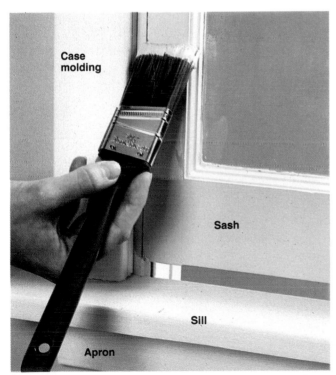

Case molding

Sash

Sill

Apron

5 Paint flat portions of sashes (1), then the case moldings (2), sill (3) and apron (4). Use slow brush strokes, and avoid getting paint between sash and frame.

6 If you must paint windows in place, move the painted windows up and down several times during the drying period to keep them from sticking. Use putty knife to avoid touching painted surface.

How to Paint Doors

1 Remove the door by driving lower hinge pin out with a screwdriver and hammer. Have a helper hold door in place. Drive out the upper hinge pin.

2 Place the door flat on sawhorses to paint. See step 3 below for painting paneled doors. Seal unpainted edges with sealer to prevent warping.

3 Let door dry. If a second coat is needed, sand lightly and wipe with tack cloth before continuing. For paneled doors, follow the correct painting sequence: first, paint the beveled edges of raised door panels; next, paint the faces of the door panels before the edges dry; next, paint rails (horizontal frame members) on the door; last, paint the faces of the stiles (vertical frame members).

Finishing the Exterior

For many remodeling projects, the only exterior completion work required is painting and caulking. Some projects, however, require more work. For example, if you have replaced an old door or window with a smaller unit, you will need to patch the exposed wall area to match the surrounding siding. Windows and doors with clad frames require exterior moldings (photo, right).

To patch lap siding, bring a sample of the original siding to your home center and match it as closely as you can. If the match is not perfect, use siding from a hidden area of your house or garage to patch the project area.

To patch stucco walls, practice first on scrap materials, because duplicating stucco textures takes some skill.

Windows and doors with clad frames have nailing flanges that must be covered with wood or metal moldings, purchased separately. This window was installed in an old door opening, which required patching beneath the window with sheathing, building paper, and siding.

How to Install Exterior Moldings

1 Cut each molding piece to length, mitering the ends at 45°. Position the molding over the window jamb and against the siding. Drill pilot holes through the molding and sheathing, and into the framing members.

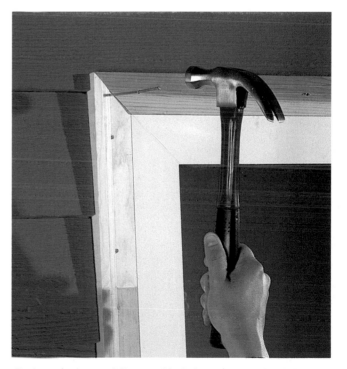

2 Attach the moldings with 8d casing nails. Drive the nails below the wood surface with a nail set. Use silicone caulk to seal around the moldings and to fill nail holes. Paint the moldings as soon as the caulk is dry.

How to Install Moldings for Windows & Doors

1 On each jamb, mark a setback line 1/8" from the inside edge. Moldings will be installed flush with these lines. NOTE: On double-hung windows, moldings usually are installed flush with the edge of the jambs, so no setback line is needed.

2 Place a length of molding along one side jamb, flush with the setback line. At the top and bottom of the molding, mark the points where horizontal and vertical setback lines meet. (When working with doors, mark molding at the top only.)

3 Cut the ends of the molding at 45° angles, using a miter saw. Measure and cut the other vertical molding piece, using the same method.

4 Attach the vertical moldings with 4d finish nails driven through the moldings and into the jambs, and with 6d finish nails driven into framing members near the outside edge of the case molding. Drill pilot holes to prevent splitting, and space nails every 12".

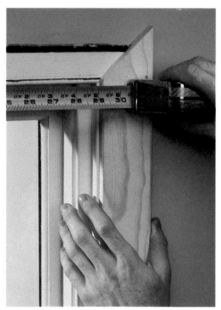

5 Measure between the installed moldings on the setback lines, and cut top and bottom moldings with ends mitered at 45°. If window or door unit is not perfectly square, make test cuts on scrap pieces to find the correct angle for the joints. Drill pilot holes and attach with 4d and 6d finish nails.

6 Lock-nail corner joints by drilling pilot holes and driving a 4d finishing nail through each corner, as shown. Drive all nail heads below the wood surface, using a nail set, then fill the nail holes with wood putty.

Index

Cowles Creative Publishing, Inc.
offers a variety of how-to books.
For information write:
  Cowles Creative Publishing
  Subscriber Books
  5900 Green Oak Drive
  Minnetonka, MN 55343